My Brain and Senses

By Paul Bennett

Silver Press
Parsippany, New Jersey

For Henry

First published in the U.K. in 1997 by
Belitha Press Limited
London House, Great Eastern Wharf
Parkgate Road, London SW11 4NQ

Editor: Veronica Ross
Series designer: Hayley Cove
Photographer: Claire Paxton
Illustrator: Cilla Eurich
Assistant designer: Sam King
Picture researcher: Diana Morris
Consultants: Elizabeth Atkinson/Jo Ormisher

First published in the United States in 1998 by
Silver Press
A Division of Simon & Schuster
299 Jefferson Road
Parsippany, New Jersey 07054

Library of Congress Cataloging-in-Publication Data
Bennett, Paul, 1954-
My brain and senses/by Paul Bennett.
p.   cm—Bodyworks
Originally published as: The senses. London: Belitha Press, 1997.
Includes index.
Summary: Describes the brain and senses and tells how they
function together to enable humans to do things like keep
their balance and remember.
1. Senses and sensation—Juvenile literature. 2. Brain—Juvenile
literature. [1. Senses and sensation. 2. Brain.]
I. Title. II. Series: Bodyworks
(Parsippany, N.J.)

QP434.B46	1997	97-6028
612.8.—dc21	CIP	AC
ISBN 0-382-39783-5 (LSB)	10 9 8 7 6 5 4 3 2 1	
ISBN 0-382-39784-3 (pbk)	10 9 8 7 6 5 4 3 2 1	

Printed in Hong Kong

Photo credits
Bubbles: 7t Geoff du Feu, 13t Jennie Woodcock, 18b Frans
Rombout, 22t Rohith Jayawardine, 25t Frans Rombout.
Mother & Baby Picture Library: 21t. Spectrum Colour
Library: 19t. Zefa/Stockmarket: 8b, 12, 23, 27t.

Thanks to models Topel, Jodie, Bianca, Meera,
Aimee, Spencer

Words in **bold** are explained in the list of useful words
on pages 30 and 31.

Contents

Your brain and senses

Your brain is inside your head. It **controls** everything you do, from turning the pages of this book, to playing games, laughing, talking, thinking, and moving.

Your brain takes in information and sends out messages to all parts of your body.

Your body sends messages back to your brain.

Some of the messages are about the things that you see, hear, smell, touch and taste. These are your five senses.

brain   skull

Your brain is very delicate. It is protected by your hard, bony **skull**.

5

The nervous system

Your **nervous system** is the link between your brain and your body.

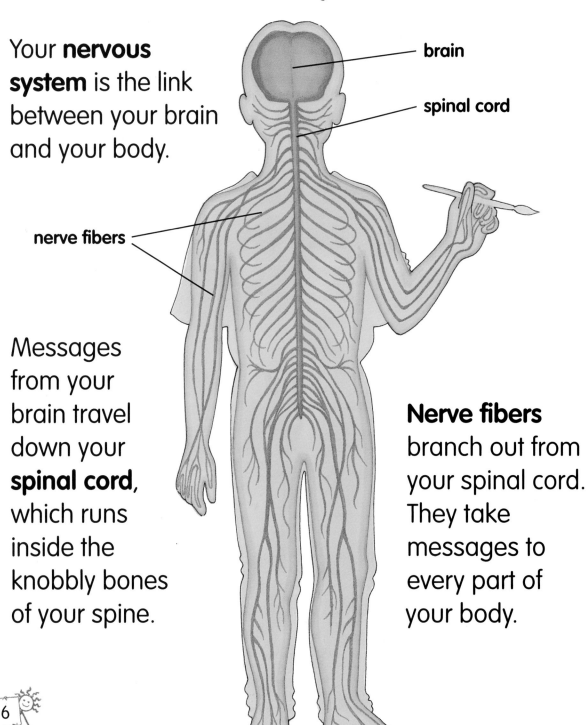

brain

spinal cord

nerve fibers

Messages from your brain travel down your **spinal cord**, which runs inside the knobbly bones of your spine.

Nerve fibers branch out from your spinal cord. They take messages to every part of your body.

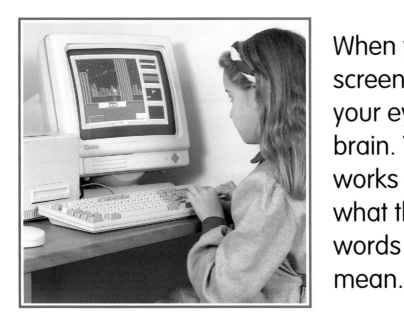

When you read a computer screen, messages from your eyes are sent to your brain. Your brain works out what the words mean.

When you paint a picture, your brain sends messages to your arms and hands to tell them what to do.

7

How do I see?

You see with your eyes. They allow you to see the world in all its different colors.

Your eye is shaped almost as round as a ball, but you can only see the front part of it. The colored part of your eye is the **iris**. The dark part is the **pupil**.

Light shines through your pupil and onto the back of your eye. Nerve **cells** in your eye send messages to your brain.

In bright light, your pupil is small to let in less light.

In dim light, your pupil is large to let in more light.

Look closely at a friend's eyes. Now ask her to cover them up. Count to ten and look at her eyes again. Do they look different?

How do I hear?

You hear with your ears. Your outer ear collects sounds, and sends them down a tube, called the ear canal, and into your head.

Inside your head, sound is turned into messages, which are sent to your brain.

Your brain tells you about the sounds you hear.

It tells you about the soft sound of a whisper, the loud sound of a car horn, the high ring of small bells, or the deep boom of a drum.

Your brain can tell you where sounds are coming from even if you have your eyes closed.

Taking care of your eyes and ears

You should take care of your eyes and ears because your sight and hearing are very **precious**.

When you are reading make sure that you have enough light.

Never look directly at the sun. Wear sunglasses to protect your eyes in bright sunshine.

If you cannot see clearly, you may need to wear glasses. One of the people who checks your eyes is called an optician.

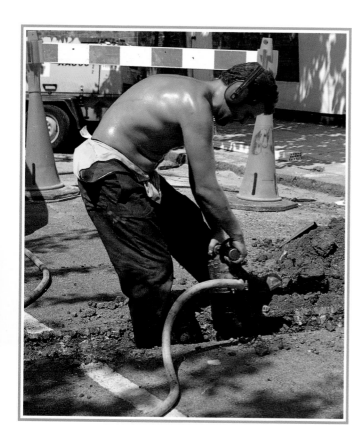

Very loud sounds can damage your hearing. People who work with loud machinery wear ear protectors that stop loud sounds from damaging their ears.

Never shout in someone's ear.

Bitter and sweet

Imagine what it would be like if you could not taste your favorite food or drink. Boring!

Your tongue is covered in thousands of tiny bumps, called taste buds.

bitter

sour

salt

sweet

Taste buds send messages to your brain about what food tastes like.

Your tongue can sense four tastes: sweet, sour, salt, and bitter.

Lemon juice is sour. You can taste it at the side of your tongue. Potato chips and peanuts are salty. These are tasted at the side of your tongue, too.

The taste buds at the back of your tongue taste bitter things like orange peel.

Chocolate is sweet and is tasted by taste buds on the tip of your tongue.

Smell

When you sniff, air goes up into your nose and messages about the smell are sent to your brain.

The scent of flowers, newly-mown grass and just-baked bread are smells most people like.

The smell of rotten eggs and unwashed socks are smells most people dislike.

When you have a cold and your nose is blocked, you have trouble tasting your food.

This is because your sense of taste and smell work together.

Hold your nose while you eat. Can you taste the food?

Touch

The surface of your skin has millions of tiny **nerve endings**. These give you a sense of touch. Your skin tells you what things feel like.

Soup is hot.
Ice cream is cold.
Tree trunks are rough.
Glue is sticky.
Slugs are slimy.
Wood is hard.

Rabbits have soft, smooth fur, which makes them nice to stroke.

18

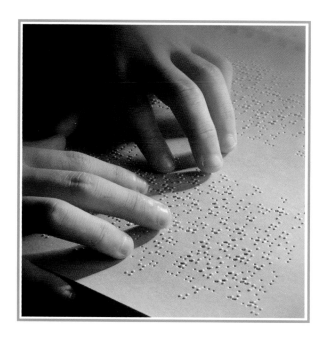

Blind people learn to read using their sense of touch. The letters are made of patterns of tiny raised bumps. Blind people feel the bumps with the tips of their fingers. This pattern of bumps is called Braille.

Apples feel hard and smooth.

19

That hurts!

Pain is your body's way of telling you that something is wrong and that you should stop what you are doing.

Your fingertips and lips are very **sensitive** to pain, and to heat and cold. They will tell you when a drink is too hot, and needs to cool down.

Elbows are sensitive, too. This mother is using her elbow to check that the water is not too hot before she bathes her baby.

When you fall over and scrape your knees, nerve cells in your skin send pain messages to your brain to tell you your knees hurt!

21

Your reflexes

What do you do when you touch something prickly, like a cactus? You pull your hand away quickly. This is called a reflex action. Reflexes are actions you do without thinking.

Babies have many reflex actions. If they are startled, they will throw out their arms to grab something.

Blinking and breathing are reflex actions, too. You can control these actions, but only for a short time.

Try this out. Hold your breath and count to 15, but try not to blink. Can you do it?

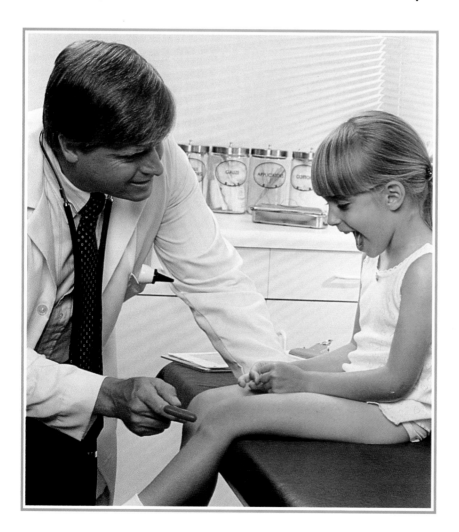

If a doctor taps your leg just below the knee, the bottom half of your leg jerks up. This is a reflex action.

Learning and memory

You begin to learn about the world as soon as you are born.

You learn to walk, talk, read, and write when you are a child.

You learn many things by doing them again and again. When you learn to write, you need to **practice** making the shapes of the letters until you get them right.

When you learn to ride a bicycle, you must practice until you can do it without thinking.

Your memory allows you to remember how to do things such as tie your shoelaces, and to **recall** facts, sights, sounds, tastes, and even feelings.

A sense of balance

Can you stand on one leg? Your sense of balance stops you from falling over.

When you move, messages are sent to and from your muscles and your brain.

Messages from your **inner ears**, eyes, **muscles** and other parts of your body help you to balance.

The messages make sure that the different parts of your body move together smoothly. This is called co-ordination.

Acrobats need a good sense of balance and good co-ordination to be able to form a human pyramid, like the one shown here.

Co-ordination allows you to throw and catch a ball, or juggle without dropping anything.

Why do I need to sleep?

Sleep gives your body a chance to recover from all the tiring things you did during the day.

Babies sleep for about 16 hours a day. A 6-year-old sleeps for 10 to 11 hours a night. An adult sleeps for about 7 to 8 hours.

Do you remember your dreams?

We all dream, but no one really knows why. Some dreams are frightening.

If you have a bad dream, think about something nice, like a party or a holiday. Soon you will drift off to sleep again.

Some **scientists** think that dreams are the brain's way of sorting out all the new information it has taken in during the day.

Useful words

Cells

Tiny parts that make up your body. All living things are made up of cells.

Controls

Directs things that happen.

Inner ears

The parts of your ear inside your head that help you to balance.

Iris

The colored part of the eye around the pupil.

Muscles

The soft, stretchy parts inside your body that make your body move.

Nerve endings

Tiny parts in your skin that tell you about the things that you touch.

Nerve fibers

Long, thin threads that carry messages from all parts of your body to your brain.

Nervous system

Nerves that branch out from the spinal cord to all parts of your body.

Practice

To do something again and again until you are good at it.

Precious

Very special.

Pupil

The middle of the eye, the part that you see through.

Recall

To remember or bring a memory into your mind.

Scientists

People who carry out investigations to find out how things happen.

Sensitive

To be able to tell the difference between things that are hot and cold, rough and smooth, sharp and soft, and so on.

Skull

The bony part of your head.

Spinal cord

A collection of nerves that run inside your backbone. The spinal cord takes messages from your brain to all parts of your body.

Index